THE RIGHT SIDE OF LEARNING

Effective Study Skills for Attention Deficit, Dyslexia, and Creative Right-Brained Thinking

A PARENT-CHILD GUIDE
BY MELANIE WEST, M.A.
Educational Psychologist

Illustrations by:

George Huante

www.georgehuante.com

PREFACE:

Why will this book help me?

Recent research on how the brain processes information has greatly influenced how parents and children can understand the learning process. Students who experience difficulties with attention, as well as students with dyslexic tendencies, share the same learning patterns as highly creative thinkers. Unconventional thinkers are bright and capable, yet may find it surprisingly difficult to succeed in school due to an overuse of Left-Brained teaching strategies.

It has been my experience, and the experience of my many students, however, that if given the opportunity to understand how the brain learns, a Right-Brained Thinker is able to approach learning in creative and successful ways.

Developing skills that keep both the left and right hemispheres of the brain consciously activated opens powerful avenues for learning. The tools in this book will help a Right-Brained Thinker improve attention, mental focus, and comprehension. These strategies will enhance organization, decrease the time needed to complete work, and increase test performance.

For a Right-Brained Thinker, it is paramount that learning feel like a deep, personal journey, and it is with that intention that this guide was developed.

This paradigm will change the lives of parents. It will provide you with a way of understanding characteristics within your child which have previously been misunderstood.

For the Right-Brained Thinker, this guide will provide a way of truly understanding yourself, your behaviors, your emotions, and your actions. You will finally be able to gain control of the learning process. Ending confusion, frustration, and careless errors, you will finally be able to learn information quickly and correctly.

This is a powerful journey, and I celebrate every curious being that has been inspired to join me in discovering pathways toward natural, authentic, right-brained learning.

Table of Contents:

Are You A Right-Brained Thinker?

If you see yourself as being a
Right-Brained Thinker, this book will:

Show you how to become good at school.

...and...

Show you how to make learning fast, fun,

visual and creative!

PART I:

Understanding how the human brain works

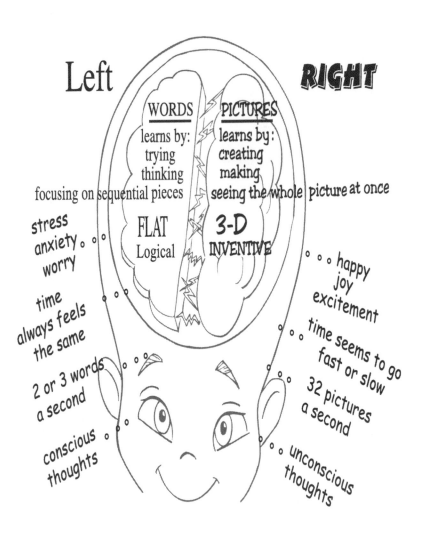

Left

RIGHT

WORDS

learns by:
trying
thinking
focusing on sequential pieces

FLAT
Logical

PICTURES

learns by:
creating
making
seeing the whole picture at once

3-D
INVENTIVE

stress
anxiety
worry

time
always feels
the same

2 or 3 words
a second

conscious
thoughts

happy
joy
excitement

time seems to go
fast or slow

32 pictures
a second

unconscious
thoughts

Brain Power

Your brain is an amazing organ. It is both simple and complex in its design. Understanding the fundamental ways the brain learns and stores information will lead to discovering specifically how your brain learns and stores information.

When you look at the picture on the opposite side, do qualities about the right hemisphere of the brain interest you?

After looking at this picture, is it even more clear that you prefer the right side of the brain?

Do some of the words in the picture already mean something to you?

Isn't it amazing that one simple picture can give you so much information?

Let's discover more about the human brain...

Man, I'm learning a lot!

Right Brain Power

The right side of the brain thinks using visual images (pictures). This part of the brain is constantly taking pictures, learning and storing information effortlessly.

The minute you were born, your brain immediately started taking pictures of your mom's face… hands… the back of her head. Your brain automatically started putting these pictures together like pieces of a puzzle. Soon, you were able to match what you were looking at with pictures that were stored in the right hemisphere of your brain. In this way, you were able to determine if the person you were looking at was someone who you were familiar with or if the person was a stranger. Comparing new pictures with old pictures is how the right hemisphere learns information.

The right hemisphere of the brain learns very naturally. It does not need to "practice" in order to learn. We do not send babies to school to "teach" them how to make pictures. We do not "force" babies to take pictures "over and over" in order to help them learn. The brain likes to take pictures, and it learns very naturally when presented with visual images.

The next thing the brain learns is to think in 3-D (three dimensions). The right hemisphere of the brain likes to imagine what might be on top, behind, inside, or underneath objects. This part of the brain understands that if you are looking at the back of someone's head, there will be a person's face on the other side. This part of the brain is very curious about what things look like, feel like, or smell like. It is curious about what an object "could" be used for and what else the object could be turned into. The brain's ability to think in 3-D allows a person to imagine what else something might be.

The single greatest difference between "humans" and other "animals" is that the human brain has an imagination.

The human brain is constantly questioning...

Who, What, Where, How...

The human brain can think through things in logical, and illogical, ways.

The human brain can imagine what "might" be the answer to the questions it is constantly asking itself.

The human brain can think about how it might create something that doesn't even exist.

The human brain really "wakes up" when it thinks about things that are not "real".

Playing with legos, action figures, or video games, watching movies, drawing, or simply staring out the window thinking about "nothing," can really feed the creative side of the human brain.

Creative thinking is the true source of learning. The ability to have creative thought allows the human animal to learn how to read, write, and do math. Developing these skills allows a person to build something that the creative center of the brain has imagined.

If you are a Right-Brained Thinker, it is very fun for you to have creative ideas. A Right-Brained Thinker often has a very vivid imagination. Your thoughts tend to become very "real".

A right-brained person likes to think about "big ideas" and the "big picture". Before you even begin to read, you like to know exactly what you are going to be reading about, how long it will take you to read it, and what will be the final outcome.

When someone is giving a long list of directions, it will be important for Right-Brained Thinkers to know *why* the list is being given to them before they can really pay attention, or listen, to the instructions.

"Where are we going?"

" Why do I need to do this?"

" How long are we going to be doing this?"

These types of questions immediately start running through a Right-Brained Thinker's mind, stopping the student from being able to really listen to the directions.

A Right-Brained Thinker may not hear important details because the brain feels distracted by its desire to know the answer to the "big" questions that are running through the right hemisphere of the brain.

Because the right hemisphere of the brain loves to think about big ideas, right-brained learners may often "know" an answer to a question but may have a hard time explaining how they know the answer.

A right-brained person may make a lot of "careless mistakes" because this side of the brain likes to think about several ideas at one time. Jumping from one thing to another makes it very hard to keep track of all the little details.

Right-brained learners easily lose their sense of time because for them time tends to move fast or slowly. It is very hard for a Right-Brained Thinker to really know for sure how long he has been thinking about something or how long it will take for him to finish a particular project.

Because this hemisphere likes to think in 3-D, the right side of the brain does not line things up in logical sequences. This hemisphere does not care about organization because organization does not help it learn.

Instead, this side of the brain likes things to have deep meaning. If you don't "like" thinking about something, it is very likely that your right hemisphere does not have a relationship with that information.

Rote, "meaningless" information that "simply must be memorized", is very difficult for the right hemisphere to accept because it lacks deep meaning. For example, some Right-Brained Thinkers struggle with

early reading skills because this requires the student to "simply memorize" many words in our language without having any real understanding of what these words actually mean. Other Right-Brained Thinkers may have a difficult time memorizing math facts because the brain is looking for deeper meaning behind the seemingly abstract equations. Information such as memorizing phone numbers, counting up and down the number line, or learning lists of vocabulary words can also be difficult for the Right-Brained Thinker if the information is not presented within a context that is deeply meaningful to the student's life experience.

Overall, the right hemisphere of the brain is an amazing place to play, think, experiment, imagine, and create. It is a powerful place for having creative, cutting edge thought. It is the place of invention. This hemisphere has the ability to make an illogical jump into a brilliant discovery. It has a drive to understand and to know "why". The curiosity of the right hemisphere makes it possible for this type of thinker to master any information that the brain finds "interesting".

Left Brain Power

The left hemisphere of the brain works in a very different way. The left side of the brain specializes in mastering language.

It thinks with "words" rather than "visual images".

While this hemisphere also begins to develop as soon as you are born, it can not express itself successfully for many years.

A baby will start "hearing" words from the moment he is born. However, most babies do not begin to say their first words until 12 to 18 months old.

The left hemisphere of the brain learns by practicing small pieces of information over and over again.

The left hemisphere helps the brain build a relationship with words. The right hemisphere of the brain knows what an object is long before the left hemisphere will be able to say the name of the object.

For example, if a baby boy feels hungry, he knows that he wants milk. But, the only "word" he has for more milk is: "WAH!!!" Over time, the baby will learn the word milk because his mother says "milk", and points to the bottle of milk, hundreds of times. It takes a long time… but the left hemisphere of the brain finally links the picture with the sound, and magically one day the baby says "milk" when he is feeling hungry.

This hemisphere likes to learn by linking small pieces of information together. It practices things over and over again, consistently getting a little better each time it "tries".

By paying attention to each little sound and putting those little sounds together, language begins to develop. First, the left hemisphere masters the ability to listen... then it starts to master the ability to speak.

Reading, calculating with numbers, and mastering the writing process are all areas that grow out of the brain's ability to process language. In order to master

reading, math, or writing, the brain must smoothly send information back-and-forth between the two hemispheres of the brain.

When you have an idea and start talking about it… the information starts in the right hemisphere and then moves into the left. You "knew" what you wanted to say. You had the "big picture" and it was "meaningful" to you… then you moved into the left hemisphere to "try" to find the "words" to express your idea.

When you are listening to someone talk, reading directions, or responding to a question, the information starts in the left hemisphere. The first thing your brain does is pay attention to the "words".

Now, the brain must move the information over to the right hemisphere to see if your brain has a picture for each of those words. If your brain links the words with the correct pictures, your brain understands the information.

If the right hemisphere does not have the correct visual images for the words, the right hemisphere will disconnect from the left hemisphere. It will feel like you "forgot" …or you got "distracted" and stopped listening. Your brain will "zone out". You may shake your head and suddenly say "what", like you just woke up from a dream. It is a very odd feeling, but if the right hemisphere of the brain can not build a visual image to match the words, your brain simply can not "pay attention" to those words.

A Left-Brained Thinker likes to line things up in an orderly, organized way. The left hemisphere likes to make sure it understands all of the little pieces before it gets started. This hemisphere likes to be very accurate and logical.

For example, while reading directions, the left hemisphere of the brain is interested in every word. If you are a Left-Brained Thinker, you like to read all of the words in the directions before you get started. The left hemisphere of the brain knows that one or two words could really change the meaning of the assignment.

A Left-Brained Thinker also has a very strong sense of time. The left hemisphere is very good at knowing how much time has passed. It is much easier for a Left-Brained Thinker to take a timed test because this side of the brain has a very good idea of how much time you have spent "thinking" and how much time you have spent working on the task.

Because the left hemisphere thinks with words, a Left-Brained Thinker is able to explain the answer to a question and will be able to express ideas in a logical, sequential way.

So... based on this information... Do you think you are a Right-Brained Thinker or a Left-Brained Thinker?

Maybe you are a mix, depending on the activity.

Think about situations where you seem to be more left-brained. Are these situations that you are good at or are these situations that no matter how hard you try you never know for sure how you will perform?

Think about situations that you approach in a more right-brained way? Are these things that you are good at or have fun doing?

What's Right (And Left) About School

In a perfect learning situation, the brain is actually sending information back and forth between the two hemispheres in a very balanced way. If information is presented to the right hemisphere first, the left hemisphere will need to kick in and help the brain organize the information in a logical, sequential way. If information is presented to the left hemisphere first, the right hemisphere will need to jump in to help the brain really understand the information and to know what big picture will be built once all the little pieces of information are put together.

Often, a student's overall performance in a classroom environment is determined by whether a student is left-brained or right-brained dominant.

Today, most of our schools are language-based systems, meaning the majority of the learning tasks activate the left hemisphere of the brain first.

Teachers in a language-based system ask students to:

- read from a textbook independently
- take notes
- spend class time doing workbooks
- spend class time doing pen and paper tasks
- take timed tests
- believe multiple repetition of materials is necessary in order to achieve mastery

Overall, these techniques work "very well" for all of the Left-Brained Thinkers in the classroom, and these techniques work "well enough" for whole-brained learners. But, this way of teaching will "hardly work at all" for a right-brained learner.

Because many of the students in the class are doing "very well" and/or "well enough" the teacher does not question his or her teaching style. Therefore, at the end of the grading period, a language-based teacher will feel confident in announcing that the students who are doing "very well" have "earned" high grades, the students who have done "well enough" have "earned" average grades, and the students that have "hardly done well at all" are "failing" the class.

To further support language-based teaching, our overall educational system encourages teachers to use a bell-curve grading system. When using language-based learning, the bell curve does in fact exist because within a group of students there will always be a mix of left-brained, whole-brained, and right-brained dominant learners.

If, however, a teacher allows students to demonstrate knowledge in a manner that fits their learning style, the bell curve softens greatly, often disappearing altogether. By providing a variety of ways to demonstrate knowledge (written test, visual representation, oral presentation) it is, in fact, possible for every child to achieve equally.

Being Taught the Right Way

For the students I teach, I present them with these questions:

What if the problem is NOT in your ability to learn...

What if the problem is that you have never been taught the RIGHT way?

"know or do not know..there is no try..."

For a Right-Brained Thinker, it is extremely important that information start in the right hemisphere.

A Right-Brained Thinker tends to be able to send information from the right to the left hemisphere successfully. However, when information is presented to the left hemisphere first, a right-brained person can shut down. Even "easy" stuff can suddenly become very hard.

When the two hemispheres of the brain stop sending information back and forth in a balanced way, a Right-Brained Thinker will experience:

- Careless errors
- Word substitutions while reading
- A blank stare when asked a question
- Difficulty understanding directions
- Inability to get started without adult support

"Trying" vs. "Knowing"

Your brain has great ability. It records every single thought you have. When you are learning something new, your brain records every success and every mistake. It records this information in the left hemisphere. This is the hemisphere of "trying" and "practicing".

One of the most effective ways to understand if you are using the left hemisphere of the brain or the right hemisphere is to ask yourself this question:

Do I have to think about the answer,

or...

Do I just know the answer?

Whenever you are "thinking about an answer", you are starting off in the left hemisphere. If you "suddenly" just know the answer, your brain shifted to the right side and retrieved the information.

One of the worst things a teacher can say to a Right-Brained Thinker is: *"Just try your best."*

"Trying" is guaranteeing that you are using the left hemisphere of the brain first. Even if you get the correct answer, you are very likely to continue to store the information in the left hemisphere, because your brain does not easily transfer information from left to right. What will happen for the Right-Brained Thinker is that he will feel very happy to have "guessed" the correct answer, but when the question is presented at a later time, the brain will act like it has never seen the information before. It will be in "try" mode once again.

It is better for a Right-Brained Thinker to remind himself that he "knows the answer" ...that he has seen the answer before. If you are a Right-Brained Thinker, it will be very helpful to close your eyes and talk to yourself in this way:

I know this answer.
I've seen this information before.
Where did I see that answer last?

A Right-Brained Thinker must learn how to visualize when asked a question. Once your imagination has been activated, the answer will flash into your mind.

The Power of Balance

When the human brain is learning easily, it is because the information is moving from one hemisphere to the other in a very fluid way.

Physical, mental, and emotional balance are all very important to a Right-Brained Thinker. When a Right-Brained Thinker is in a left-brained situation, he must be very careful to consciously keep in mental balance.

When information stops crossing over to the opposite hemisphere, a Right-Brained Thinker will:

- *lose attention,*
- *be physically or verbally impulsive,*
- *make a careless error.*

Therefore, it is important for a Right-Brained Thinker to have successful strategies that will help keep information jumping back and forth between the two hemispheres.

Understanding The Power of Creative Thought

For a Right-Brained Thinker, creating a visual understanding of a concept is essential. The authentic learning style of the right hemisphere must be satisfied in order for the brain to truly understand the information. The brain may be able to listen to the word; it may be able to use the word in a sentence; it

may even be able to read and write the word. However, right-brained learners will only be able to think with the word if they create a visual image that accurately represents the meaning of the word.

Therefore, the single most important thing a right-brained learner can do is to use his creative instincts to build visual images for words and concepts.

I often ask students to "show" me their understanding of a word. This can be done by having the student build a visual model, create a picture, or act out a scene that illustrates the student's understanding of a concept.

When a concept (or word) seems particularly difficult, I will encourage the student to build a visual model (with clay or other materials) of what the word really means. Building a 3-D model is by far the best way to employ the right side of the brain. When language (left-hemisphere activity) is expressed in 3-D form (right-hemisphere activity), a right-brained learner moves from a state of "trying" into a state of "knowing" the information.

It is my experience that creating visual models for a key concept is the most accurate way to assess what elements of a concept have been mastered and what elements remain vague or unknown.

It is important for Right-Brained Thinkers to visualize and then verbally describe their ideas for a model before drawing or building begins. As a Right-Brained Thinker is encouraged to put words to the creative vision, a picture in the imagination will become more clear. This also allows time for the adult and student to add to, or expand on, the concept. It can be emotionally difficult for a Right-Brained Thinker to add to, or change, the model after it is completed, because this evokes a feeling of having "done the model wrong" and thus discourages the learner.

Building visual images or dimensional models allows the Right-Brained Thinker to experience conceptual mastery. The brain can now truly "think" with this word. After having done this with several concepts, the brain will begin to consciously build models within its imagination.

Over time, a Right-Brained Thinker will not need to build every conceptual model. A right-brained learner can become a fast effective learner, simply by being able to quickly identify concepts that have been mastered (concepts that activate his imagination) and concepts that cause the imagination to go blank.

When a word or concept can easily be visually retrieved, the student does not need to "study" that information. The Right-Brained Thinker need only place his attention on building images for concepts that are missing a picture.

When a Right-Brained Thinker has a creative thought, the thought can feel very "real". Once a right-brained learner is consciously engaging this aspect of the brain, learning suddenly becomes very fast and intensely interesting. The natural born learner emerges. Suddenly the Right-Brained Thinker begins to soar through the left-brained world of academics... learning information the "right-brained" way!

PART II:

Right-Brained Learning Strategies

(that really work!)

Discovering Mental Focus

It is really powerful for a Right-Brained Thinker to become aware of an idea called Mental Focus.

In the biggest sense, Mental Focus is when your brain and your body are both paying attention to the same information. Athletes often refer to this feeling as being in the "zone". When you are in Mental Focus, the brain is only paying attention to what the body is doing. There are no competing thoughts. No mistakes can be made because the brain is placing all of its thoughts on the task at hand. This type of focus is so relaxing for the brain that most people will describe it as feeling like they are not thinking at all... only doing. When the brain has a single point of focus, all possible distractions completely fade away.

When I introduce this concept to a student, I start by asking my students to think of themselves as being two separate people.

*One part of you is called **Physical Me**.*

*The other part of you is called **Mental Me**.*

Physical Me is all the elements that represent your body. This includes all the ways your body looks and all the things that your physical body can do.

You can run, jump, read, listen, draw, play… everything your body can do represents the idea of Physical Me.

Mental Me, however, represents all the things that you can think about… all the things you can imagine… and all the things you can create in your imagination.

Try this:

☐ Close your eyes and reflect inward. Say the words Mental Me to yourself and see what happens. You may be flooded with an emotion. You may see a bright color or an unexpected picture in your mind. Because Mental Me is an abstract idea, every person will experience this differently. However, you are very likely to immediately understand that Mental Me has a lot more power and freedom than Physical Me.

☐ Mental Me can think and imagine anything!

Physical Me vs. Mental Me

Physical me is reality-based.

While Physical Me can do many things, it has to "wait" until it is allowed to do these things, and it is limited by whether it actually has the skill and ability   to do what you are thinking about.

It is easy to know where Physical Me is.

If you are sitting across from me, I am looking at your Physical Me.

Mental Me is imagination-based.

Mental Me is only limited by your imagination.
Mental Me can think about anything it wants to
any time it wants to. Sometimes you will know
what Mental Me is thinking about, other times you
will simply feel like you are daydreaming or zoning
out.

It is very difficult to know where Mental Me is.

I could be sitting across from you... looking
straight at you... talking to you... but Mental Me
could be thinking about something very different
from what I am saying.

You could be sitting in class, "listening" to
the teacher, but Mental Me is thinking about
Disneyland... or playing after school... or
wondering about a sound that is outside the door.
This list can go on and on because Mental Me has
the ability to put its attention onto anything that
you might be curious about.

When Physical Me and Mental Me Are Not Working Together

For a Right-Brained Thinker, it can be very difficult to control Mental Me. Your brain loves creative thought. Your brain loves to feel free to think about whatever it is curious about.

When Mental Me dominates, the brain is no longer capable of processing outside information correctly.

Physical Me will hear someone talking, or be looking at a piece of paper... BUT... if Mental Me is not putting its attention onto the same information, a Right-Brained Thinker will:

- *miss the information*
- *feel spaced out*
- *respond incorrectly*
- *get started in the wrong way*
    ...or...
- *feel utterly lost!*

Mental Me Controls
Your Experience

Mental Me is the part of you that really controls what you are thinking about. Mental Me controls what you are really experiencing.

For a Right-Brained Thinker there are times when Mental Me is thinking about what is "really" going on: Mental Me and Physical Me are paying attention to what the physical eyes are looking at or what the physical ears are hearing.

However, it is equally possible that Mental Me is having a creative thought and that thought is stopping the brain from paying attention to what the physical eyes are looking at or what the physical ears are hearing.

For a Right-Brained Thinker this can be very unsettling. You may feel like someone "really" told you something or that you "really" thought you were doing the right thing. But, your teacher (or your friend or even your parent) is saying to you that you are "wrong", that what you thought is not "real".

Because it is difficult for Mental Me to know what is "real" and what is "imagined", a Right-Brained Thinker can easily become withdrawn, bored, upset, frustrated, distrustful or mad.

For a Right-Brained Thinker, creative thoughts will override any information Physical Me is sending to the brain. What Mental Me is focused on is very real to the brain. What Mental Me is focused on absolutely controls what you believe to be true.

Getting Control of Mental Me

B ecause the right hemisphere of the brain loves to have creative thoughts, Mental Me can really grab onto this and play... play... play!

For a Right-Brained Thinker, Mental Me is extremely active.

So... if you want to have the ability to hold your attention or if you want to feel extremely focused on a particular task... then you've got to find a way to control Mental Me.

All of this is to say... it's time to start really understanding yourself. Understanding Mental Me is the place to start.

Discover your Mental Me and start having a relationship with it by asking yourself:

Where is Mental Me?

How do I feel when Mental Me and Physical Me are not working together?

How do I feel when Mental Me and Physical Me are working together?

Snap out of it!

While it can be very difficult to really know what Mental Me is thinking about, it can be very easy to recognize when Mental Me has packed up and left Physical Me behind.

Becoming interested in controlling Mental Me is the gateway to effective, fast learning.

Although it is difficult to control Mental Me's desire to focus on distracting thoughts, you can develop the ability to pull Mental Me back into Physical Me any time you want.

When Mental Me is fully connected to Physical Me, your brain feels relaxed, focused, connected, and fully awake. I call this "being in the moment" because Mental Me is truly focused on what Physical Me is doing.

There are two simple tools that will help you "snap out" of a distracting thought and re-connect to the present moment. I call these "Let Go" and "Connect".

Let Go

L et Go is a simple relaxation technique. It is actually a very natural way for your brain to decompress. When a basketball player stands at the free throw line, or a tennis player prepares for a big serve, or a swimmer anticipates jumping off the starting block, notice that each of them takes a deep, deliberate breath. By doing this, the two hemispheres of the brain activate equally, information comes into the brain accurately, and Mental Me puts its entire focus on what Physical Me is doing. The eyes focus solely on the target, the brain "lets go" of thinking and the body springs into action. The athlete knows that it is essential to let go of all distractions in order to gain a single point of focus.

The following is a way to practice the idea of Let Go:

Try This:

☐ Close your eyes and visualize a small empty space in the middle of your head.

☐ Take a deep breath, and when you exhale, allow the small empty space in your head to expand and grow.

☐ Open your eyes, and allow yourself to feel mentally relaxed... imagine the muscles in your forehead opening up and relaxing.

☐ Allow yourself to feel like everything is "starting fresh"... like you are just waking up for the first time.

☐ Every time you feel spaced out, zoned out, distracted, or confused, remind yourself to

"Breathe"... and "Let Go".

Connect

Next, you will want to find a way to pull Mental Me into the present moment.

If your mind is feeling blank, if you feel tired or bored, foggy or stressed, it is because Mental Me is being distracted by a thought that does not match what Physical Me is doing.

Whenever you make a careless error, feel distracted, or feel like you "just can't think," it is because Mental Me is NOT in the present moment. Mental Me is no longer connected to what Physical Me is looking at or listening to.

This is where you get to use your creative ability. In order to regain the connection between Mental Me and Physical Me, you must design a visual image that will help you "feel" Mental Me re-connect. By creating a visual image, you will stimulate the right hemisphere of the brain in a more conscious way which pulls your mental attention back into your awareness. My students describe their mental image for Connect in various ways. For some, they visualize and feel a small amount of weight resting on their physical shoulders which brings their attention back into the present moment. Others describe feeling like Mental Me and Physical Me "click" back together like two pieces to a complex puzzle twisting back into place. Some students will say that a foggy feeling leaves their heads, and they suddenly feel

much more clear-headed. Whatever your experience is with Connect, it must be something that is very real to you. The visual image you use for Connect is the one thing that will absolutely pull your mental attention back into focus. Connect is a very powerful, unmistakable feeling.

When you choose to Let Go and Connect, you will notice that you are now consciously aware that Mental Me had gone away, but now you are "back". You will immediately feel more clear-headed. The light in the room may seem brighter and more clear. Your body will feel like it just got a boost of energy. Your brain will feel like it's just now looking (or listening) to the information. Your attention and focus are back and ready to be put to good use.

As you continue to play with the idea of Let Go and Connect, you will see how much faster the learning process is when Mental Me and Physical Me are really working together.

Have fun practicing pulling yourself into the present moment when you are feeling uncomfortable, bored, tired, or spaced out.

Enjoy playing with your newfound ability to control your attention and your ability to experience true focus.

Discovering your Learning Power

Understanding how the brain works will help you discover more specifically how your brain learns information. It will allow you to learn more quickly and make it easier to "check-in" with yourself to make sure you actually *know* the new information.

THE RIGHT SIDE OF LEARNING

You can significantly speed up your learning rate by consciously building visual images.

As you read (or listen) to someone speaking, take time to close your eyes and imagine a blank screen in your mind. Ask yourself:

Could I draw a picture of this information?

You will notice that if you allow yourself to talk softly aloud, or talk to yourself in your mind, the picture will become more real. Allow yourself to add important details, so that the picture is fun, interesting, and accurate.

It is generally easier for the brain to create visual images for fun, dynamic words. Essentially, all the things you like to think about are things that are fun for you to visualize. However, new vocabulary words and new concepts can be extremely difficult to visualize.

When the brain is unable to create a visual image for a word, the brain experiences a blank screen.

If you have too many blank screens while reading something or listening to someone, Mental Me will not be able to stay focused on the information. When this happens, a Right-Brained Thinker may:

■ jump to conclusions,

■ interrupt the person speaking,

■ stop reading and look ahead in the book,

■ space out or start daydreaming,

■ lose his place while reading,

■ make word substitutions while reading, or

■ look around to see what others are doing

A Right-Brained Thinker may even keep reading, working, or listening, but at some point you will realize that you have not been following along, and you now have no idea what is going on.

To learn key concepts and new vocabulary words, it will be important for a Right-Brained Thinker to have resources for developing the correct visual images. Discussing possible pictures with another person or finding good sources for visual images will become essential for building a strong foundation for learning new information.

There are two main reasons why a Right-Brained Thinker may not understand something:

(1) Your brain can not build a visual image to match the information, or

(2) Your brain is focused on the wrong picture, and your thinking process is now stuck.

Wrong Picture

The bus went flying down the street.

The single fastest way to turn on your Learning Power is to start checking whether you can "visualize" a picture that illustrates what the information really means.

The more you play with this, the stronger your picture-thinking will become. You will quickly begin to notice that you can memorize and recall information much more quickly simply by creating strong visual images.

Study with Visual Cards

A n effective way for a Right-Brained Thinker to study is by creating a visual matching game using the new vocabulary words (or new concepts).

Try This:

☐ Place a vocabulary word (or keyword for a new concept) on one card. On another card draw a strong visual image that embodies the meaning of the word, include one or two key words on this card (making sure you have a good visual understanding of each of these words) in order to be able to visualize these words in association with the word written on the other card.

☐ Use Visual Cards when studying "facts," such as

> Vocabulary lists
>
> Terms and Definitions
>
> Math Facts
>
> States and Capitals
>
> Math terms and formulas

☐ When your study cards have been completed, play mix and match games with as many study cards as possible. When you look at a particular card, ask yourself if you can "visualize" the matching card in your imagination. The more frequently you talk to yourself AND activate your visual imagination, the faster information will be mastered. When you are able to match all word cards with the correct visual images... studying is complete. You are ready to take the test. You might be surprised at how quickly you can do this. I have many students that master large amounts of information almost as quickly as they design the study cards.

Visualize your Answer

While taking a test, a Right-Brained Thinker should find a concept that was on a study card... stop reading the test question... look away from the paper and visualize the study card to recall all key elements... now, continue reading and answering the test question.

Pulling up a picture of the answer in your imagination before you start to read the answer choices or before you begin to write the answer is an extremely important strategy for the Right-Brained Thinker. Because the right hemisphere is not "good with words", a Right-Brained Thinker can be easily tricked by the way test questions and answer choices are written.

It is also extremely helpful for Right-Brained Thinkers to put their pencils down while visualizing an answer. Holding a pencil automatically activates the left hemisphere of the brain and can block the brain from activating the right hemisphere.

If a written response is required:

Try This:

☐ Allow yourself to see the main answer in your mind and visualize the answer resting on top of a table.

☐ Now... ask yourself... what are the "legs" for this table... what supports my answer?

☐ For shorter answers, add two supporting elements to the answer (add two legs to the table), for longer answers add additional supporting elements (additional legs to the table image).

☐ This process is done BEFORE beginning to write any part of your answer.

(Note: If you do not like the Table Visualization, you can create another image. However, I encourage you to discover one image that works for you and stick with it so that the strategy becomes a tool that you use automatically when presented with a question.)

Get Moving

While studying information... Get Moving! Physical movement can help the brain move information from one hemisphere to another.

Physical movement helps to keep the right-hemisphere of the brain activated while learning. Talking aloud about new ideas and concepts while engaged in a physical activity will assist in helping the brain build a stronger conceptual understanding.

Try This:

☐ Walk around the block visualizing and talking yourself through the information.

☐ Study while bouncing a ball back and forth.

☐ Use your imagination! For instance, you might visualize points on a basketball court and place specific information in certain places. While taking a test, you will be able to re-activate this visual image and just "see" the answer sitting there, waiting for you to use it.

☐ In my work with students, I have found it incredibly effective to have the student sit on a Yoga Ball instead of a chair. The physical balance that is required to stay on the ball demands that Mental Me stay in the present moment. If you try this, notice that you may suddenly start leaning against a wall, or using something to help you control your balance. This is a sign that Mental Me is starting to pull away from Physical Me, but before it took off it wanted to make sure that something else could be used to keep you in balance. This is such a simple technique, but it will amaze you as to how much better your attention and focus is just by sitting on a balance ball.

Working Backwards

This is another learning strategy that will amaze you!

Many classroom assignments (and questions in a text book) are designed to prompt logical, linear, sequential thought (all left-hemisphere processing).

The idea behind this is that if the student builds on each of the steps, in the end he will have the big picture.

It's like "understanding" the project is the reward at the end of a long journey.

Unfortunately, many Right-Brained Thinkers need to know the Big Picture *before* the brain can think about any part of an assignment.

If you are looking at an assignment and the "answer" does not immediately come to your mind,

Try This:

☐   Allow yourself to focus on the last element of the problem (or the direction) first. Make sure you know where the assignment is going and that you've got the big picture.

☐   If possible, do the last (or most fun) elements first.

☐   Stimulate and satisfy the right hemisphere by doing the creative elements first.

Checking for Visual Pictures

W hile listening… reading… or studying information, the single most important thing a Right-Brained Thinker can do is to check for Visual Pictures.

Try This:

☐   *Close your eyes if you need to,*

☐   *Coach yourself through the thinking process,*

☐   *Ask yourself:*

"Can I see a picture to illustrate this information?"

This alone will change everything about the learning process. You will quickly be able to zero in on missing pictures. Building and creating powerful images for complex concepts will allow you to think at a high level without getting tricked by the words. This is a powerful, fun, fast, and incredibly effective learning strategy.

Be playful. This way of learning is highly creative. "Boring" class work can suddenly become fun and entertaining to think about. Activate the imagination and open up a whole new world of learning through picturing words.

PART III:

Why is it hard for me to visualize some words?

Why is it hard for me to visualize some words?

Whenever it becomes difficult for you to visualize a word (or concept), it is because your brain is missing the picture that represents what the word really means.

You may often find that looking a word up in a dictionary does not really help you. Even if you are able to read the definition, you may not understand the word any better than you did without the dictionary.

For a Right-Brained Thinker it is essential that you can see how that word would fit into the real world. The word must be experienced and placed into a meaningful context. It will be very helpful for you to have someone you

trust that can help you see how that word would work in your world.

Be aware that this not only happens with words that are new to you, but also may be happening with what you would consider "easy" words.

Because a Right-Brained Thinker only understands words that make a visual image, any word that does not activate a matching picture will be dropped during the "thinking" process, potentially impacting reading and listening comprehension.

For Example:

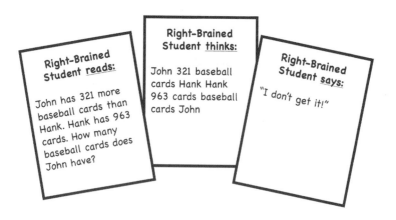

Right-Brained
Student reads:

John has 321 more
baseball cards than
Hank. Hank has 963
cards. How many
baseball cards does
John have?

Right-Brained
Student thinks:

John 321 baseball
cards Hank Hank
963 cards baseball
cards John

Right-Brained
Student says:

"I don't get it!"

Why is this happening to me?

One big obstacle for a Right-Brained Thinker is that in early elementary school students are asked to memorize (without having meaning) the top 200 most used words in the English language (referred to as Sight Words).

Rote memorization of these words is considered an essential step along the road to "learning" how to read. With a fair amount of work, many Right-Brained Thinkers will eventually be able to "read" these words... but they are left unable to "think" with these words.

The teacher feels accomplished because the student can read a passage aloud (even though the student may continue to substitute and/or misread some Sight Words). However, in future grades, reading comprehension scores, understanding directions, and higher level writing skills will remain weak.

What can I do about this?

In order to work well within the left-brained world of school, a Right-Brained Thinker must develop a deep relationship with language.

To get started on this path, I encourage students to develop a meaningful understanding of the Sight Words. These are words that the student has read thousands of times yet still has a weak understanding of what these words really mean.

The following is an example of how a Right-Brained Thinker may master an understanding of the Sight Word "a".

First, the student is presented with a general understanding of the word:

- The word "a" is letting you know that one thing is being talked about.

- But, it is not just talking about a number. The word "a" is also telling you that there is more than one to choose from, and in this case it does not matter which one you choose to picture.

- So, the word "a" tells you that you can picture "any one".

Next, the student is asked to create a visual image that represents the deeper meaning of the word "a".

In this case, the student visualizes a bunch of bananas with one banana being focused on… "any one".

The following is an example of how a Right-Brained Thinker may master an understanding of the Sight Word "the".

- The word "the" is telling you that the thing (or things) being talked about is important or special in some way.

- If you are reading the word "the", you must ask yourself: "Do I know which one the author is talking about? Do I have the same picture?"

Now, the student is asked to create a visual image that represents the deeper meaning of the word "the".

In this case, the student visualizes "the boy".

The crown and the dog bowing down remind the student of the idea that the Sight Word "the" tells you that the boy being talked about is special or important in some way. You have to know which one to picture.

Mastering Sight Words

In order to master the Sight Words, Right-Brained Thinkers, must reflect within themselves to seek a personal understanding of the word. It will be very helpful for the Right-Brained Thinker to work with an adult to help clarify and expand understanding of these words.

I encourage my students to start with these 20 words. However, remember that there are approximately 200 words in the English language that are considered Sight Words. After mastering these top 20, I would encourage any Right-Brained Thinker to continue to explore other Sight Words. As language opens up into rich, colorful pictures… suddenly a Right-Brained Thinker experiences the depths of authentic learning. Weaknesses fall away as true understanding emerges.

Top 20 Sight Words

a	this	what	am
the	that	why	was
of	where	be	their
to	here	is	were
from	there	are	been

For more help visit
www.TheRightSideofLearning.com

Emotional Balance

The last element of the Right-Brained Thinker that I want to touch upon is the connection between right-brained dominance and Emotional Intelligence.

The right hemisphere of the brain is wired to be very "feeling" oriented. It is creative and intuitive. The right hemisphere is interested in how color, sound, smell, and textures make the brain feel.

A right-brained learner can be "overly" sensitive to foods, lighting, clothing, noises, voice tones, and environmental spaces. The extent to which these sensitivities affect the Right-Brained Thinker varies greatly from student to student. As stress builds, any sensitivity will become more intensified.

On the plus side, a Right-Brained Thinker is often very insightful, compassionate, and creative.

Physical, Mental, and Emotional Balance are essential to a Right-Brained Thinker. Developing routines that strengthen a sense of balance and well-being are paramount in keeping a right-brained person an effective learner. Reducing left-brained work, increasing creative time, and providing routines that promote emotional and physical balance are essential.

Keeping the "big picture" in mind is an important place to start. For a Right-Brained Thinker, staying focused on skills that promote success in life keep the learner tapped into the broader purpose for learning.

Making School-World Better

As a Right-Brained Thinker it will be important that you constantly look for ways to make "school-world" work better for you. Most academic tasks will be structured to favor the left hemisphere of the brain. However, with a small amount of creativity, any task can be approached in a right-brained way. These few strategies will help you along the way.

For a Right-Brained Thinker:

   ✳ Learn to type.

   ✳ Learn how to ask for help. Ask and receive help joyfully.

   ✳ Learn how to help yourself. Use tools to support learning: a calculator, an electronic spell checker, dictation devices, and computer images to develop pictures for key concepts.

   ✳ Learn how to make even the most boring tasks fun and creative.

   ✳ Learn how to identify your weaknesses and create a support system to help you in those areas.

   ✳ Learn how to twist left-brained tasks into right-brained activities.

* Learn how to "switch on" the right hemisphere when you are feeling bored, tired, confused, or discouraged.

* And most importantly, have fun learning how to learn the "right" way.

Melanie

My name is Melanie West. I am an Educational Psychologist in Southern California.

I'm a Right-Brained Thinker.

The first five years of my professional career, I worked as a school psychologist for public schools where I conducted neurological testing on nearly a thousand students age 3 through 18. By the time I moved into private practice, I felt like I had "seen it all."

While working for school districts, I attempted to successfully navigate the waters of Special Education. Seldom did I feel victorious. I loved every child that crossed my path, yet felt at the deepest level, that the "system" had let them down. I left my position with public schools and embarked on a journey to discover a paradigm that would REALLY work.

For the past 10 years, I have been witnessing the powerful effect of right-brained learning strategies. The results are consistent and amazing. I thank my beloved students who have so joyfully guided me into the world of right-brained thinking.

For a personal consultation regarding your child's needs, please visit
www.MelanieWestLearning.com

Want to see the Right Side of Learning
strategies in action?

Looking for additional ways to support
your Right-Brained Thinker?

Log on to:

www.TheRightSideofLearning.com

Made in the USA
Charleston, SC
22 March 2010